MW01127271

Networking,

It's Your

Superpower

By Kesha Kent, BA, MAOL

Gabriela!
Thank you!
Blessings
Kesha

Copyright © Kesha Kent

All rights reserved. No part of this book may be reproduced in
any form or by any electronic or mechanical means, including
information storage and retrieval systems, without permission in
writing from the publisher, except by reviewers, who may quote brief
passages in a review.

ISBN 978-0-578-72070-8

Library of Congress Control Number 2020941521

Editing by Stella Joy

Book Design and Front Cover Image by Patrice Gardner

Printed and bound in the United States of America

First Printing July 2020

Published by Dean Diaries

To order additional copies of this book, contact the author:

Kesha Kent

mrskeshspeaks@gmail.com

https://mrskeshspeaks.com/the-book/

Table of Contents

Dedication

This book is dedicated to my first love, my soul mate, my amazing husband. He has been my biggest support! Thank you for listening, cheering, and, most importantly, reminding me that everything is aligned correctly. To my daughters, thank you for growing with me while figuring out life. You all are my biggest accomplishment. Remember, girls; the sky is not the limit; it's just the view!

The whole JOURNEY BEGINS here

About the Author: KESHA- pronounced as (Keesha)

During this journey of writing my first book, there were several opportunities to gain new skills, so I would start and then stop! An essential thing I now know is that the timing is always perfect! Every experience I have gained over the last 20 years has prepared me for my book release! Walking through the life of a serial networker and recovering people-pleaser has been somewhat of an awakening. Eventually, I grew to a height I never imagined, and today in 2020, I am now ready to release *Networking- It's Your Superpower*. I am grateful for this extraordinary process!

Meeting new people is my thing, and when our spirits connect, almost instantly, I recognize there's magic! I was able to take note of these gifts. I initially recognized them in high school. At that time, I was in search of love and my true identity. That caused me to become everything for everyone else, not taking into account the massive changes that were occurring in my life!

During this time I had just moved away from everything I had known at that time, I moved from St. Louis. We moved to a completely new zip code, which was over 500 miles away! This is where the traumas of my life invaded the space of creativity inside me, and the journey to find myself began! I'm so grateful for every interaction, every friend, and every connection. All these added value to me, and I can look back today and say THANK YOU. It was all part of the bigger, greater process! My next book will cover more of my journey and how it all molded me, stay tuned.

Introduction

Over the last 20 years, I found that it's easy for me to engage, connect, and meet new people! I am in the Human Resources/ Recruiting World, where I have worked with Hiring Managers and Candidates from every walk of life. Including, Engineers, Information Technology rockstars, Occupational Therapists, Nurses, amazing salespeople, and everyone else in between. Recruiting has always been my way to explore outside of my zip code and my experience level. I learned so much by asking questions and connecting with the SMEs (subject matter experts)! Early in my career, I met so many talented recruiting leaders who taught me how to listen, take notes, and ask many questions! Therefore, I asked questions. It's such a gift of mine. I've mastered it. I've recruited and interviewed individuals with PHDs as well as entry-level individuals. We all want to be heard, and that is the key to connecting with people! Listening!

In this book, I shall share the ways by which I have connected with different people, in numerous settings, and have made AMAZING connections. Which have allowed me to grow as they sparked from volunteering and attending events just once! It has always been my goal to meet at least one new connection and truly build a lasting relationship! ALL IN!

Lastly, I want you to remove any negative impression you have had in the past relating to networking. Get rid of it. Say this, "Networking truly is my superpower." Let me make this as easy as possible. My goal is to help you see past that first encounter. In this book my goal is to provide essential tips and tools to help you understand that you have the power to create lasting and effective relationships! This will also help you execute your game plan successfully! Now you'll have the cheat codes to the game of networking, which is essentially connecting and building relationships.

CHAPTER 1

Your START Is The Key

Quick Note: Whether you enjoy networking like me or you dread it, allow me to share practical/realistic tips to make connecting fun, and this will, in turn, form lasting relationships that you will value! Each time I give a talk, share with a group, or connect with anyone in person or virtually, I always make it known that it all starts from the moment that you decide what you want! Networking is no different; we must decide what we want. Start from:

1. New partners for business, career, leisure

2. New clients, customers

3. New relationships/friendships

4. New business partners

5. New investors

6. New mentors and sponsors

7. New opportunities, speaking engagements

C H A P T E R 2

Authenticity

Commonly, people cringe hearing the word 'network.' Sometimes, they feel uncomfortable networking or even feel awkward, just walking up to strangers to start a conversation. It is like any other learning curve that requires practice as well as time and attention. Moreover, you need to understand your value and be sure to show up to add value. Do not hesitate to give first, and then watch how it wonderfully comes back!

In any setting, coming armed with your goals, your elevator pitch, and your passion are the key factors to attaining your aim. Actually, you might not know what you are passionate about, just take a few days, ask the people you have worked with and check the skills and functions that are easily done by you.

First off, set your intentions, and then create the goals that you would be looking forward to achieving. The essence of setting these goals is to tell you to what extent you are productive and effective when it comes to building that new network. Your goals should be SMART, yes, SMART (Specific, Measurable, Approachable, Realistic/Relatable (to you), and Time Specific). State your aims and objectives before you attend each networking event, whether you are in person or virtual!

For instance, "While attending Venture Cafe, St. Louis, I would like to connect with three SEO Specialists who can assist in developing my website marketing strategy by July 1, 2020." Once you create your goals, allow them to work for you, and help you gauge ultimately, which direction is best for you to go! Use the process of elimination as you try specific ways to connect and be OK with pivoting as needed!!! I will say this several times throughout this book; it's a gradual process, and like any other relationship, it takes time to build! It's NOT a one-nightstand!

CHAPTER 3

Examples of Real Experiences

I am a proud graduate of Judson University in Elgin, Illinois, Class of 2005 and 2014! I have obtained my Bachelor's in Management and Leadership, as well as my Master's degree in Organizational Leadership. Oh yes! Judson had prepared me at the early stage! In early 2000, a seed was planted when I met a Career Counselor at Elgin Community College. She shared that there was a Networking Open House at Judson (it was a College then). We sat down, mapped out a plan, set goals, estimated the probabilities, and lastly prepared me adequately for attending my first real networking event! The following day, I attended Judson College's Open House, and I was immediately drawn in. One of their Academic Advisors, Jill Smith, truly connected with me! She greeted me at the door and welcomed me warmly

As Jill would say, there were others, but she STOOD out! We spoke that evening as if there were no one else in the room. She listened to my concerns, and I made it known to her that I didn't really have a path that I wanted to pursue! Jill absorbed that information and placed me in the path of obtaining a Bachelor's degree! She made me leave that evening feeling like I could conquer the world! She answered all my questions, and my wheels started turning right then and there!! She was very pivotal in my decision to soar and become a Judson eagle! She believed in me the more and wanted me to achieve my goal, the moment I started contemplating obtaining a Master's degree, I reached out to her! She shared with me that Judson was offering an online Master's degree in Organizational Leadership. Due to her cordial relationship, I couldn't help but say yes to starting school again after being out for almost ten years. Relationships matter!

After my classes began, I immediately began networking in my cohort. Our group consisted of eleven men and women from all over the Midwest and the country. They also enrolled to start the Bachelor's program. There were so many different perspectives, cultures, backgrounds, as well as familial statuses ranging from mothers to fathers, and grandparents. The good news is that we had one thing in common, we ALL sought better futures, and Judson College was the vehicle we chose! We connected based on geographic location, recipes, culture, motherhood, sisterhood, business sector, industry, and of course, our classes as well as assignments, group projects, and a natural desire to succeed. We left any differences outside of our cohort. It was like a code of honor! I didn't practice, didn't write it down, nor did I think twice about it! It all happened spontaneously, and I loved every bit of it. Looking back on it now, molded me into the diverse individual that I am. Joining the team of leaders, who were in pursuit of excellence, changed my life.

Our cohort met every Wednesday and Friday evenings from 6-10 pm and one Saturday a month for 20 months! We stayed together for the duration of the Management and Leadership program. We created so many amazing bonds and friendships which at the heart happened merely because we opened our hearts to connect! My journey of becoming an engaging speaker and serial networking guru began to materialize right there on the campus of Judson University in Elgin, Illinois, in 2003!! Well, honestly, it's where I discovered my gift of winning others over (WOO). My favorite class amidst others was Communications and Public Speaking. I thrived in these classes, and I was a natural. I also had amazing instructors, who led me, guided me, and reminded me not to say "Um" or "Ah." All you have to do is simply pause and gather your thoughts, then move forward in grace. I'll never forget those lessons!

Later in our program, one of the assigned books-The Strengths Finder by Tom Rath was introduced! It's a must READ and so amazing at helping hone your skills and abilities! This helps with every aspect of networking! Pick it up! Thank me later!

Mentoring/Careers Networking

One of my first positions out of high school was working at Sherman Hospital; I worked in the Telemetry Department. I reported to Shirley George, who subsequently was from the same city that I was from, St. Louis, Missouri! While writing this book, I had to stop and find her on LinkedIn, and who would have guessed, she's back in St. Louis as well? Lunch soon, after all of the quarantine life ends, of course!

During my interview, I remember how thorough she was, professional, well-groomed, and so intuitive.

Our interview sparked something in me; I saw myself in her. She was not only the head of the Department of Telemetry; she was BOLD and held her own. About a week later, I was offered the position, and I became her Administrative Assistant! This was my first big girl job! I learned so much from Shirley, she was so outgoing and had such charisma, it was infectious! I remember attending meetings, taking minutes, scheduling meetings, and managing her calendar. Our one-on-one meetings were such a boost for me personally and professionally. I will never forget how helpful she was in connecting me with other leaders within the organization!

She was a gift to me, and watching her in her element inspired me in ways I could have never dreamed! I now realize that it was all part of the plan. I was able to sit under a strong, professionally savvy woman who reminded me that I could be one too; be a leader!

Fast forward to 2020; I reached out to her to share my desire to include her in my book! Who would have guessed she resides in St. Louis? All thanks to the possibility of being able to re-connect by using the power of virtually connecting with LinkedIn.

My message read:

Hello there!!! I hope you are well? I once worked at Sherman Hospital in Elgin IL in the Telemetry Department, for a Shirley George... did you work in the Illinois area at one point? Your face looks familiar. Actually, the only thing I remembered about Shirley George I worked for is she was from St. Louis just like me!

Her response:

Hi Kesha, yes, I am Shirley George, who previously worked at Sherman Hospital in Elgin, Illinois. Are you in St. Louis? I can be reached at 314-XXX-XXXX8.

I am looking forward to hearing from you.

I share this as a reminder; networking can be super easy, make the first move, set your goals, and ask for the relationships you would like to have!!! Take these steps toward building strong networks and relationships.

BLANK INTENTIONALLY

"Winners are not afraid of losing, but losers are. Failure is part of the process of success. People who avoid failure also avoid success."

-Robert T. Kiyosaki, Rich Dad, Poor (Book)

The truth about networking events

It is time I broke this down! We often arrive at events virtually and in person and see how clicks are already formed! I want you to walk away from the people you already know and have a plan of action to connect with others. It will help you build a sustained network. It takes discipline and, of course, a plan. We tend to go to networking events with people we know or meet up once we arrive. It's great to have introductions made and then walk away! This is the opportunity to allow new relationships to begin, with the two people you have connected! I have found a few connections at networking events. Here is why; the format of the event, the layout of the event, and the intentions set are not conducive to meeting new people!

Out of all the networking I have been involved in, the most fruitful connections I made came from a handful of mastermind groups. The groups naturally attract people with similar interests to me. These are people that I'm guaranteed to not only get along with but connect with on a deeper level. Joining groups such as the National Human Resource Association, Professional Alliance of Women,

20

Professional Organization of Women, and Toastmasters Clubs, have helped me tremendously! Whether it's a swimming club, copywriting group, or a yoga retreat--the important thing is that it contains a group of like-minded people who you can easily bond with. Here's my advice to anyone looking to grow their network; only join groups that interest you. Never join groups or go to events with the sole intention of networking or "making connections." That is a waste of your time. THINK about building relationships!

Your top priority and #1 goal should be to merely build new relationships and remember that everything is RELATIONAL!

"If you want to go quickly, go alone. If you want to go far, go together."

-African Proverb

CHAPTER 4

Tools To Help You Connect

Whether you are networking in person or virtually, we have the internet readily available, and using these tools is simply an advantage you have to leverage your relationships!

To begin, here are a few tools to use when connecting:

LinkedIn: LinkedIn is most relevant for the workplace and has tools that make it great for business networking specifically. For example, not only can you see someone's resume, skills, and references, you can as well use a publishing platform to syndicate content there. And, most importantly, you can find common connections.

-Eden Chen of Fishermen Labs

GroupMe: GroupMe is a fantastic way to build relationships and stay connected. It allows you to self-select your group and quickly create a meaningful community. It's free, works on any device, and can even be used over text messages. It has helped me tremendously! Roshawnna Novellus of Novellus Financial

Eventbrite: Nothing beats face-to-face networking and communications. Eventbrite is a powerful way to stay apprised of local industry events. Attend them when possible, whether small or large, to allow yourself the opportunity to meet and connect with new people. Virtual connections are great, but at the end of the day, having face-to-face encounters is much more powerful.– Marcela De Vivo of Gryffin

Those are just a few tools, and as you strategize your plan and purpose, it will all come together beautifully. I want to remind you that each relationship takes time to cultivate, and once you begin to recognize viable relationships, it will help you become even more confident!

Building on Linkedin is one of the most valuable things I have ever done. It is a platform that I gained amazing relationships! Earlier in 2019, I reached out to the Campus President at my alma mater, Judson University, and I expressed interest in speaking to the students, staff, and partners. I shared a little bit of my journey as well as my "Networking, it's your Superpower" presentation, that I've shared in several locations all over the Midwest! After reaching out, he responded and thanked me for reaching out, then connected me with his assistant. We later connected, and she scheduled a Skype meeting with him. Our conversation was indeed a Godsend. We connected already on LinkedIn, and I have been following the Judson page, as well as his page!

He connected me to the Director of Development, and the rest is history! During Homecoming 2019, I was the speaker at the Network Night and Homecoming Speaker at our annual Chapel for Homecoming! They rolled out the red carpet; I was welcomed back to campus, where I have not been since I graduated from my Master's of Organizational Leadership program. This all was made possible by merely reaching out to make the ask! I share this as a reminder, what do you need to simply ask for and expect the results will be in your favor?

"If you don't ask, you don't get!"

-Stevie Wonder

CHAPTER 5

It Is All About The FOLLOW-UP

Immediately after meeting your new connection, send an email, LinkedIn message, or whatever means you choose to communicate by simply saying, "Thank you!" Do this within the first 48 hours! Because doing so will keep you top of mind! Now, if by chance you're well past the 48-hour mark, apologize for the delay, mention what you talked about and offer your skills and expertise!

Example: *Hello Eddie, it was so great meeting you a few months back at The Regional Arts Commission Gala, during the time we discussed your need for a Receptionist.*

Although some time has passed, I want to share an amazing individual who just relocated to the area. I've included her resume and contact information. Please, let me know if I can assist in any way!

Once they respond, then think of the next phase! The next thing to do is to ask to meet for an introduction call, Zoom, lunch or coffee, to connect further!

Example for sales, after an initial event or pitch: Hello Michael, Hope you are well? I wanted to follow up on our conversation. You mentioned that you'd like to have your new website up and running by the end of the year. I've pulled a few sample marketing plans and designs I'd love to share. Let's grab a coffee or schedule a Zoom meeting. I'm available Thursday at 3:15 pm, or Wednesday at 8:15 am, please, let me know which is better.

I am looking forward to connecting! Take great care.

"The key is NOT to prioritize what is on your schedule, but to schedule your priorities!"

-Steven R. Covey

CHAPTER 6

Providing Value Is The Key

1. Be willing to offer your service/expertise:

If you are a hairstylist, nail technician, massage therapist, or makeup artist, you can offer a discount coupon or a gift certificate for your services. This is a WIN-WIN for everyone involved! You will get to show off your skills and build a new client/network at the same time.

2. Share their content:

Connecting to your new contact on social media is an excellent opportunity to share their business with your network. If they have a blog or an article they have written, take time to read it, and repost it to your social media platforms, be sure to tag them.

3. Make an introduction:

If you think someone in your network could benefit from connecting with someone else in your network, you could shoot him or her a quick message saying something like:

"I noticed you're looking to break into the speaking industry. I'd love to introduce you to Kesha Kent. She works as an Event Planner in L.A., and I am sure she would be a valuable addition to your network. Would you be interested in getting an introduction?"

4. Share an article you have read:

One of the easiest ways to start a conversation or stay in touch is always to offer value. Send them a quick message and say something like this; I saw this article and thought of you! I wanted to share. Enjoy! This will cause you to be top of mind, and they'll remember the gesture!

CHAPTER 7

Ready, Be Set and Go; Take Action

Now, it's time for you to take action! Understand that nothing will happen unless you start taking action. Are you looking to advance in your career? Are you looking for an investor? Are you looking for speakers for your organization? Are you looking for new clients? Are you looking for business partners? Are you looking for customers? Here's the common denominator in all of these scenarios, people work with people they trust and have a relationship with! It doesn't matter if you change companies, switch up your products or move to a new area, people that trust you and have a relationship with you will join you every time!

I suggest you start with a guide for building relationships. Remember, it is all about your follow up, which should occur within 48 hours!

Sample message:

Hi Emma,

      It was so great meeting you at Venture Cafe last Thursday. I appreciate the information that you shared in your presentation, I left feeling so empowered and have signed up for your next presentation. I'd love to connect further over coffee. I'm available Wednesday 5/7 or Monday 5/12 at 9:00am.

Looking forward to connecting!

Have an amazing day,

Kesha Kent

mrskeshspeaks@gmail.com

linkedin.com/mrskeshspeaks

314-XXX-XXXX

Follow up after a purchase has been made: This can be sent via social media or email!

> Hi Kesha,
>
> I wanted to personally thank you for your purchase! You're going to love my new white tea candles. I'm excited for you to give me a review. Here is the link to do so: bitly.com/go
>
> After you review I'll enter you in my drawing to win more candles!
>
> Please follow me on IG and FB @candlegirl.
>
> Have an amazing day!
> Tina Turner
> CandleGirlWorld

Sample Follow up Spreadsheet:

Event/Date	Event/Date	Event/Date
Jane Doe, ABC Company Email, phone	Jane Doe, ABC Company Email, phone	Jane Doe, ABC Company Email, phone
Contacted ✔ Emailed Connected ✔ mm/dd/yy	Contacted ✔ LinkedIn Connected ✔ mm/dd/yy	Contacted ✔ Facebook Connected ✔ mm/dd/yy

Keeping this cheat sheet will help you maximize your network! This is a simple version, but you can truly use all the bells and whistles! The key is "FOLLOW UP!"

Now It's Time to Use Your Superpower

Make a list of people that you plan on connecting with.

What skills/expertise will you offer someone else?

What skills/expertise are you looking for in someone else?

Who do you need to follow-up with?

List the goals you plan to accomplish with your connections?

Lastly, I would like to thank you for joining me as we build relationships all over the world. I'm here to help and can't wait to hear about all the amazing relationships being formed! To those who have already joined my journey, thank you for being in the Networking Tribe!

If you are looking for more tips and pointers on Networking, join me on Facebook, in my group "Networking, it's your Superpower" private group!

Book me for speaking, hosting, and emceeing:

mrskeshspeaks@gmail.com

www.mrskeshspeaks.com

Tune in to my podcast:

https://anchor.fm/MrsKeshSpeaks

Networking- It's Your Superpower

Anchor, Spotify, iHeartRadio, Google Podcasts, Breaker, Pocket Cast, Radio Public